A COLORING BOOK

I Love Butterflies

Coloring Book

Jose Valladares

This edition published in 2021 by Circlesquare Projections

ISBN: 978-1-7369559-6-3

Circlesquare Projections Publishing Company Pacoima, CA, 91331

Table of Contents

Introduction

Butterflies are insects, and most butterflies have bright colors. You will get a chance to color beautiful butterflies. It is easy to color these beautiful insects; helps you learn their names, and improves your creativity.

You will find 50 beautiful illustrations. One design per page to prevent colors to bleed through.

You will need the following supplies:

- Crayola pencils or prism color colored pencils premier

- Blending pencils - helps you blend colors together

- Pencil sharpener

- Brush tip markers

- A storage container for storing all your supplies

It is easy and fun to color these butterflies designs and I hope you enjoy coloring these pages.

Have fun!

Spicebush swallowtail

Pipevine swallowtail

Beautiful morning

Queen butterfly

Mexican bluewing

Monarch

Royal butterfly

Arizona sister

Common buckeye

Marpesia petreus

Spring

23

Vanessa cardui

Eastern pine elfin

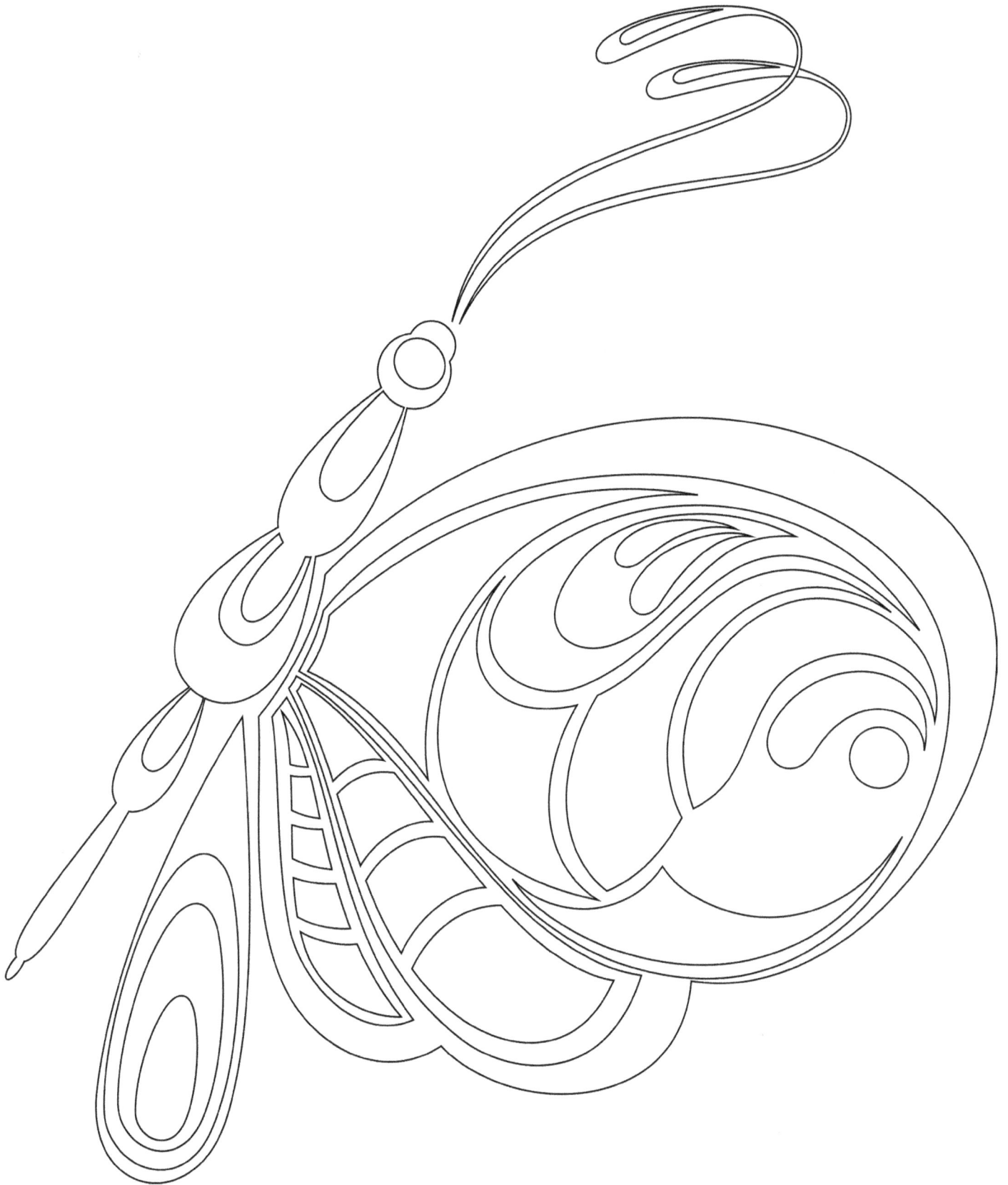

Peacock

Ringlet

31

Large white

Canadian tiger swallowtail

Love and peace

37

Red admiral

Papilio troilus

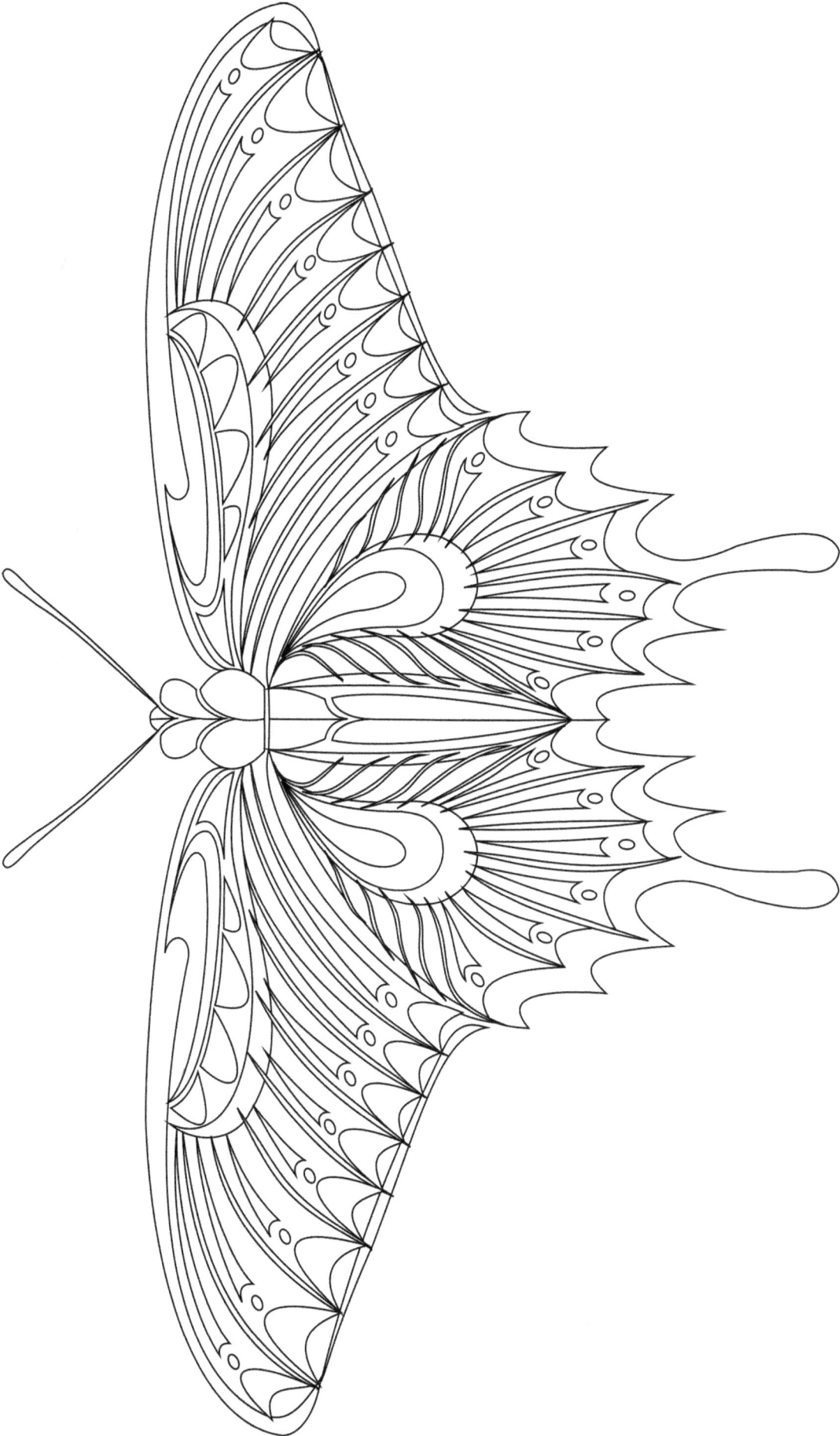

Egyptian butterfly

Wooden butterfly

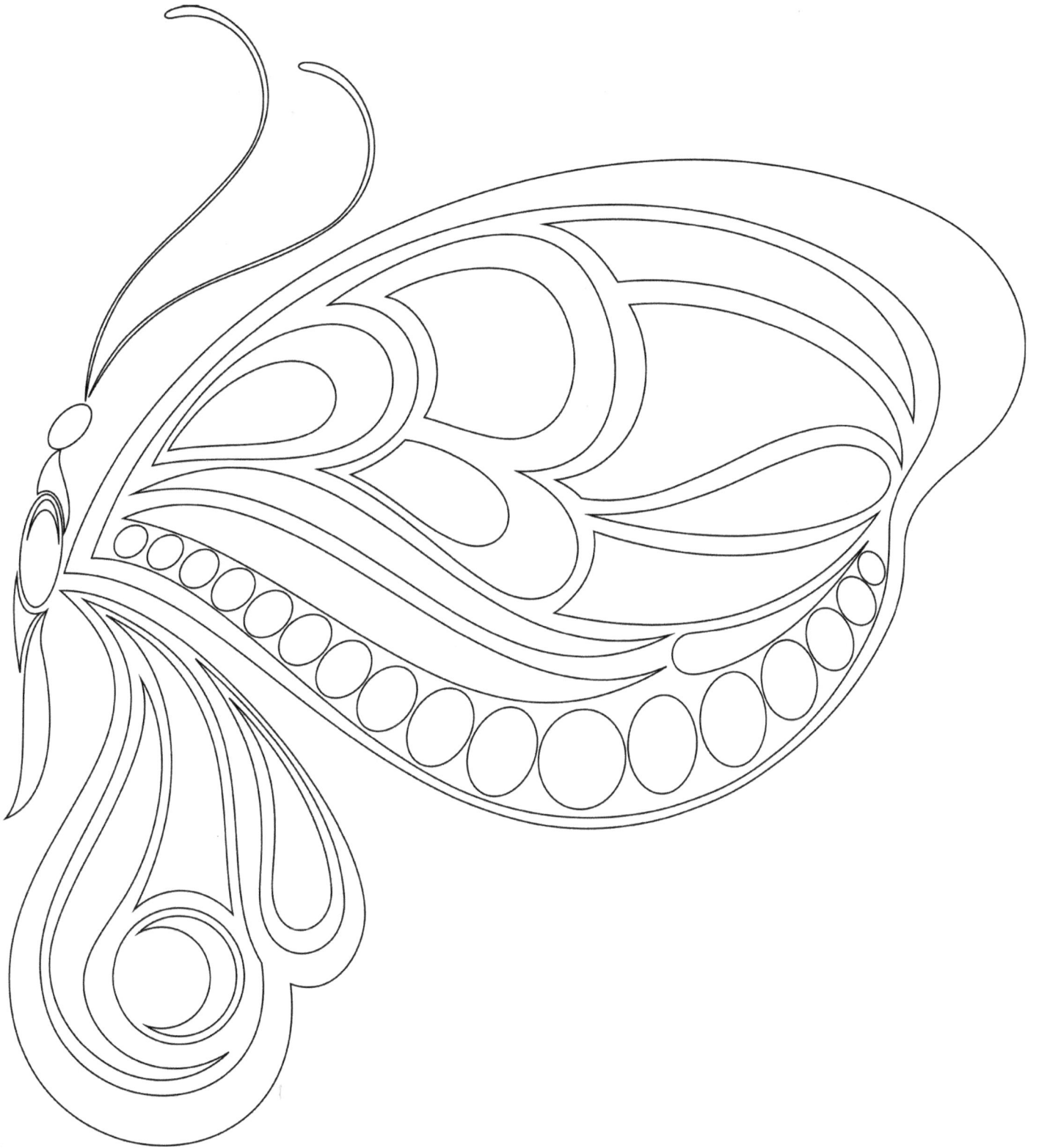

Resting

American copper

Spring

51

Lovely time

Best friends

Black swallowtail

Silkmoth

Colorado hairstreak

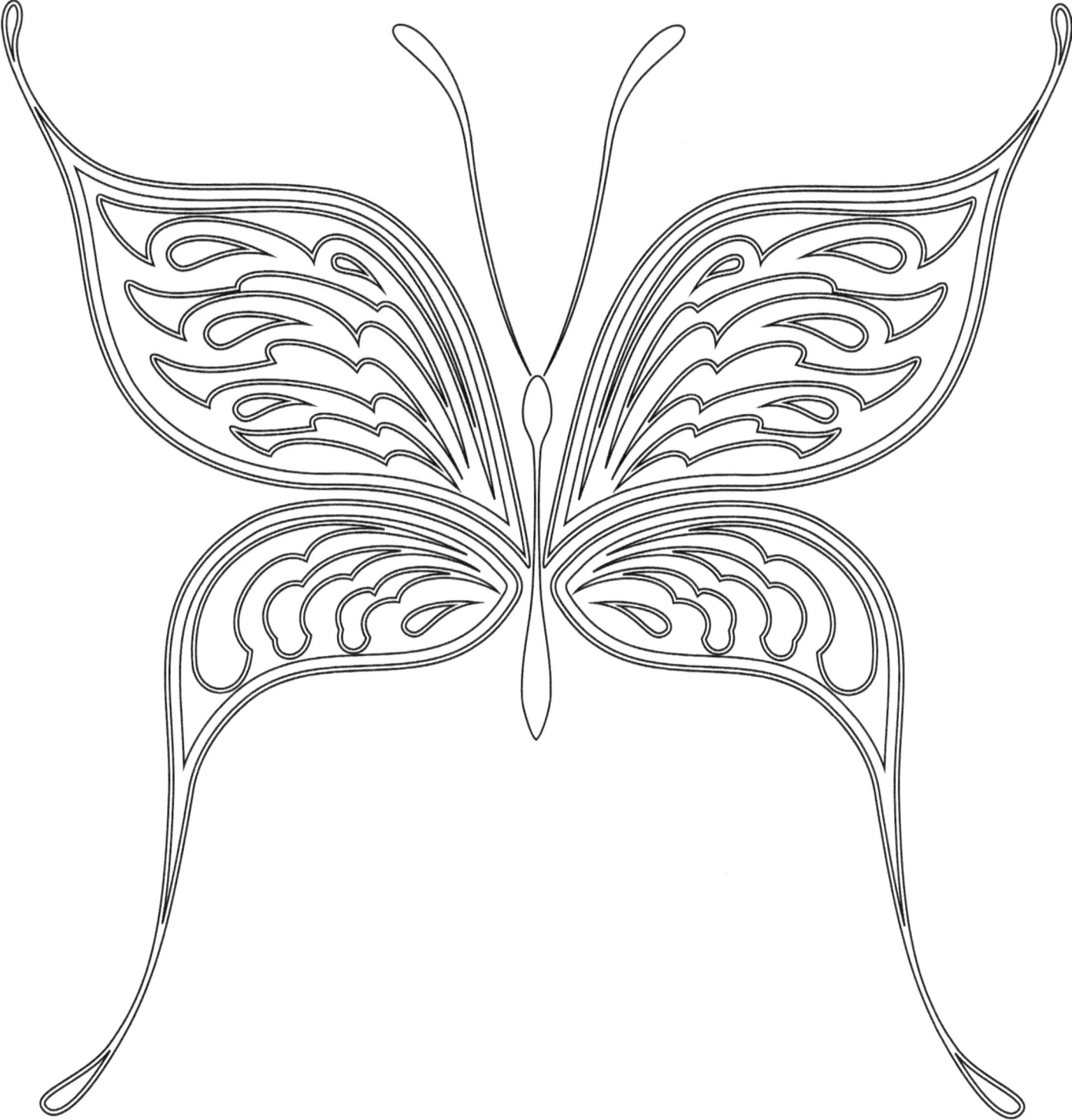

Chrysina gloriosa

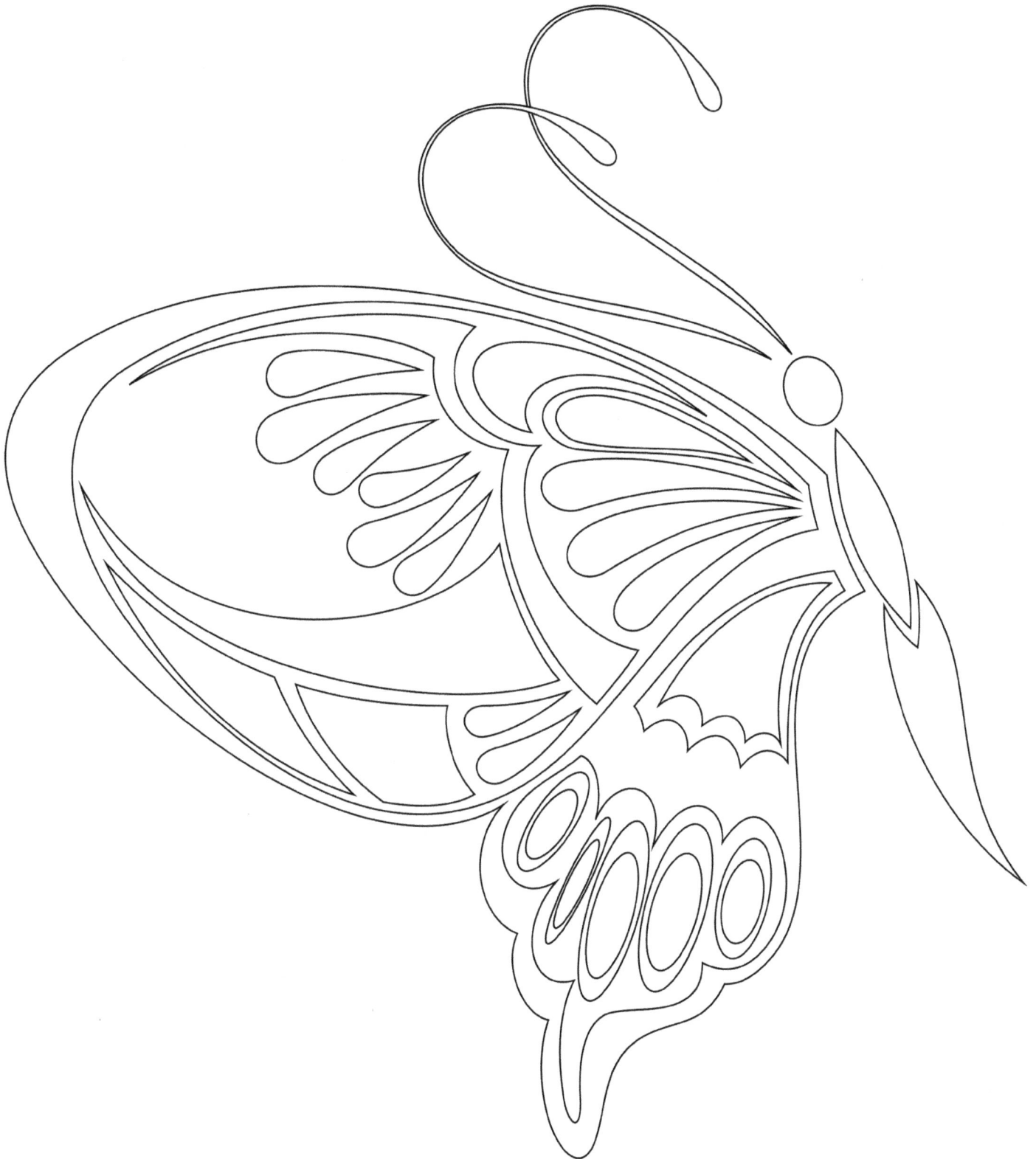

Indian swallowtail

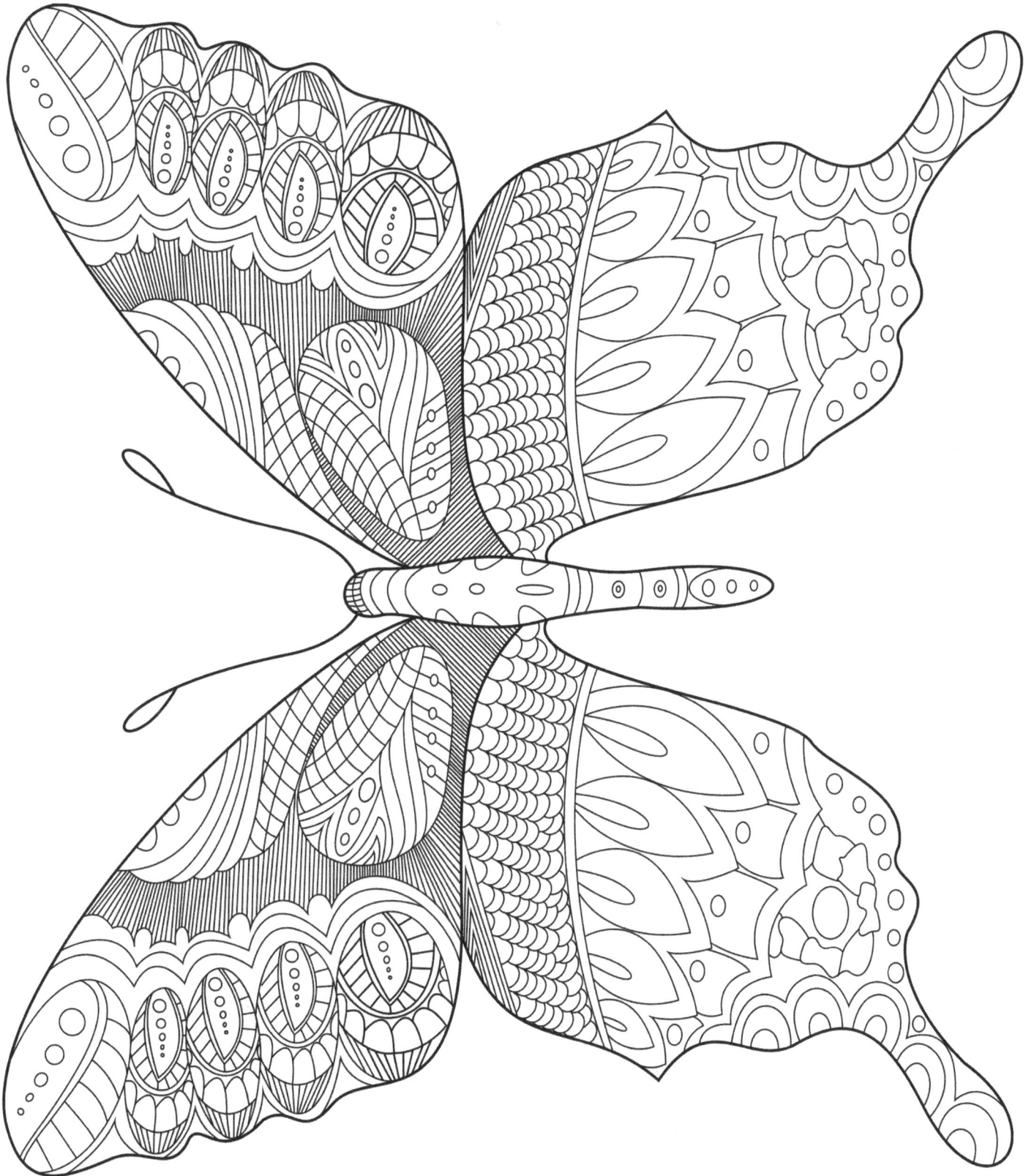

Brimstone

Golden butterfly

Silver studded blue

Marbled white

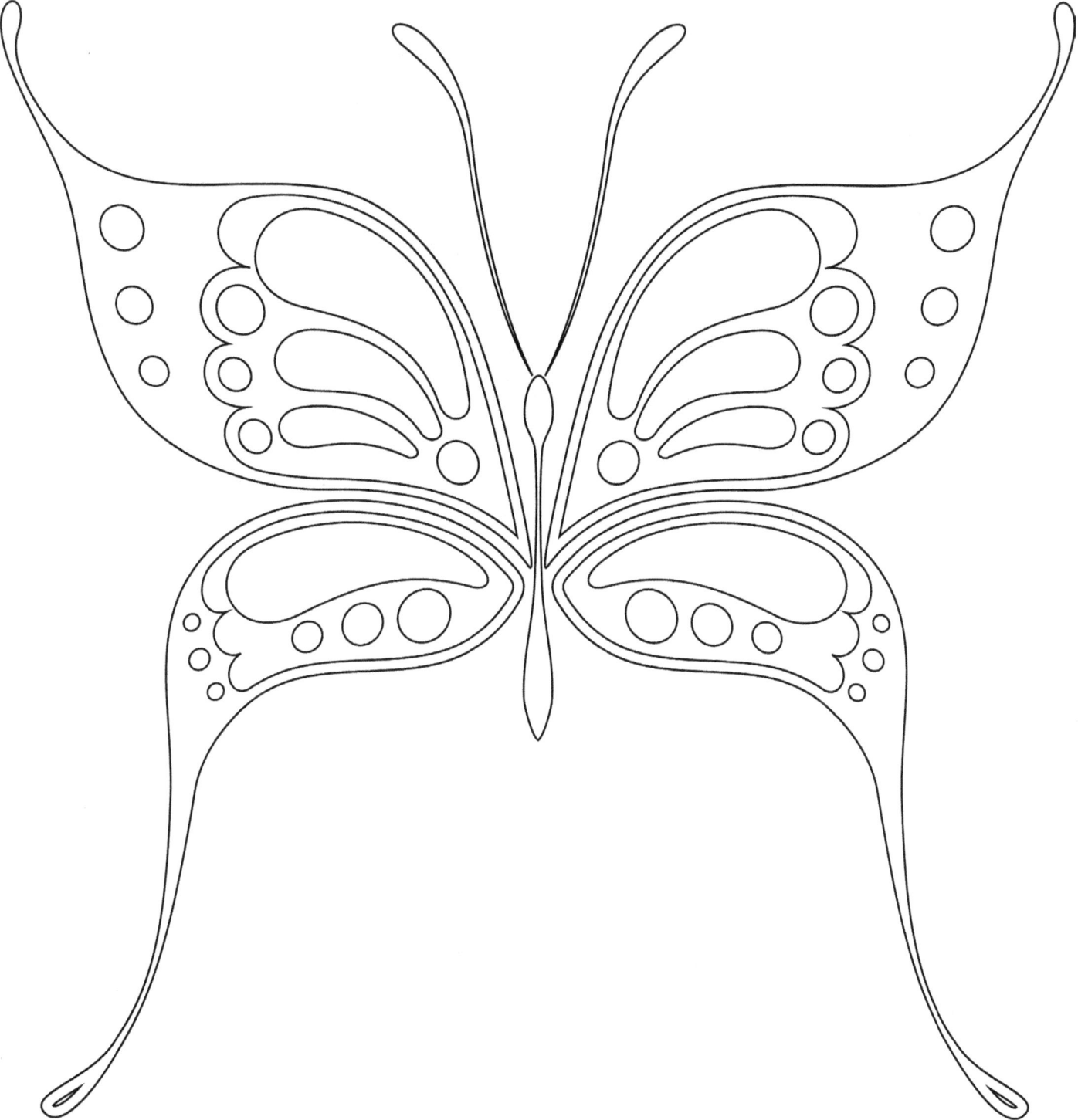

Sara Orangetip

Red-spotted purple

Megisto cymela

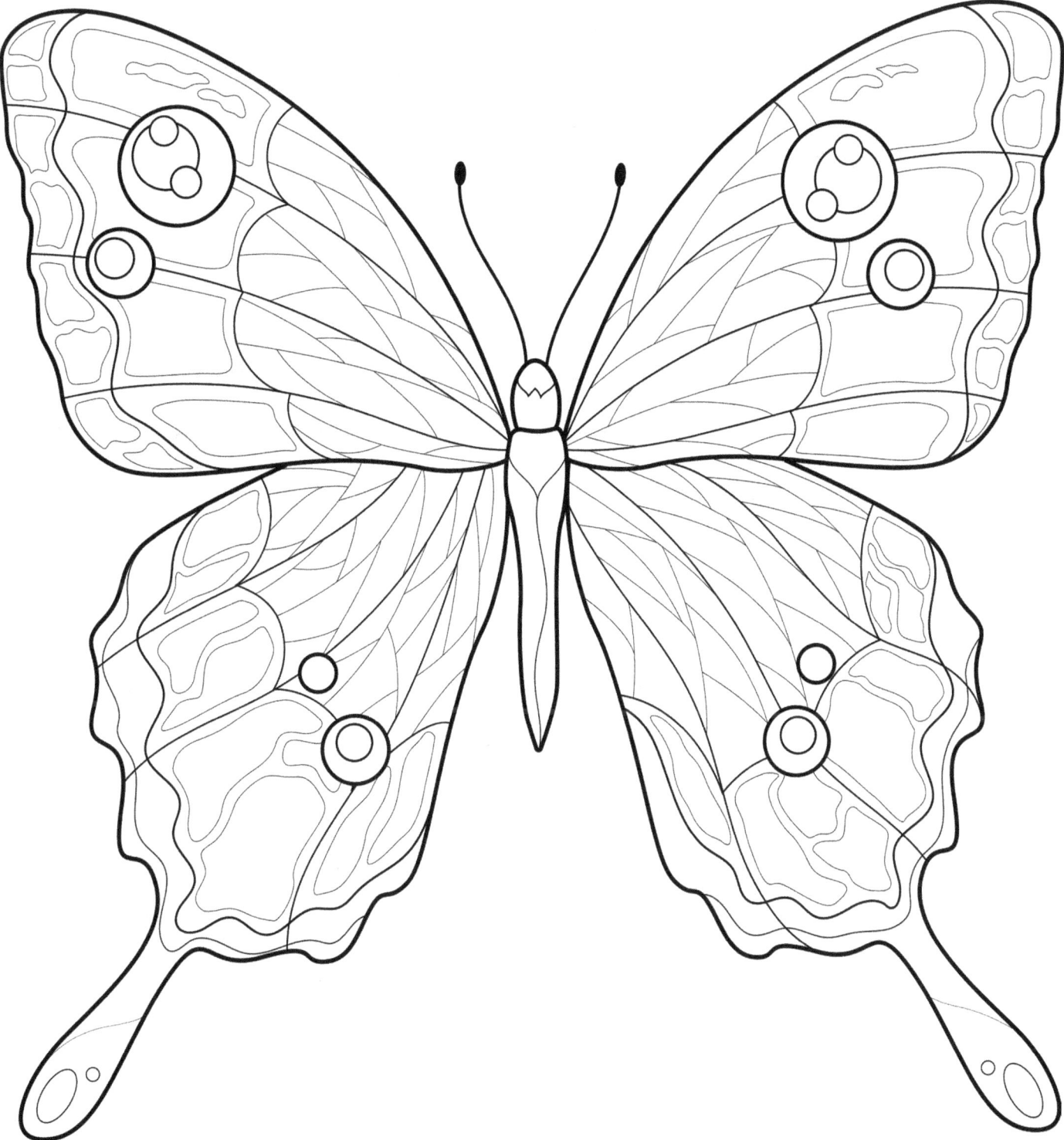

Purple emperor

Marpesia petreus

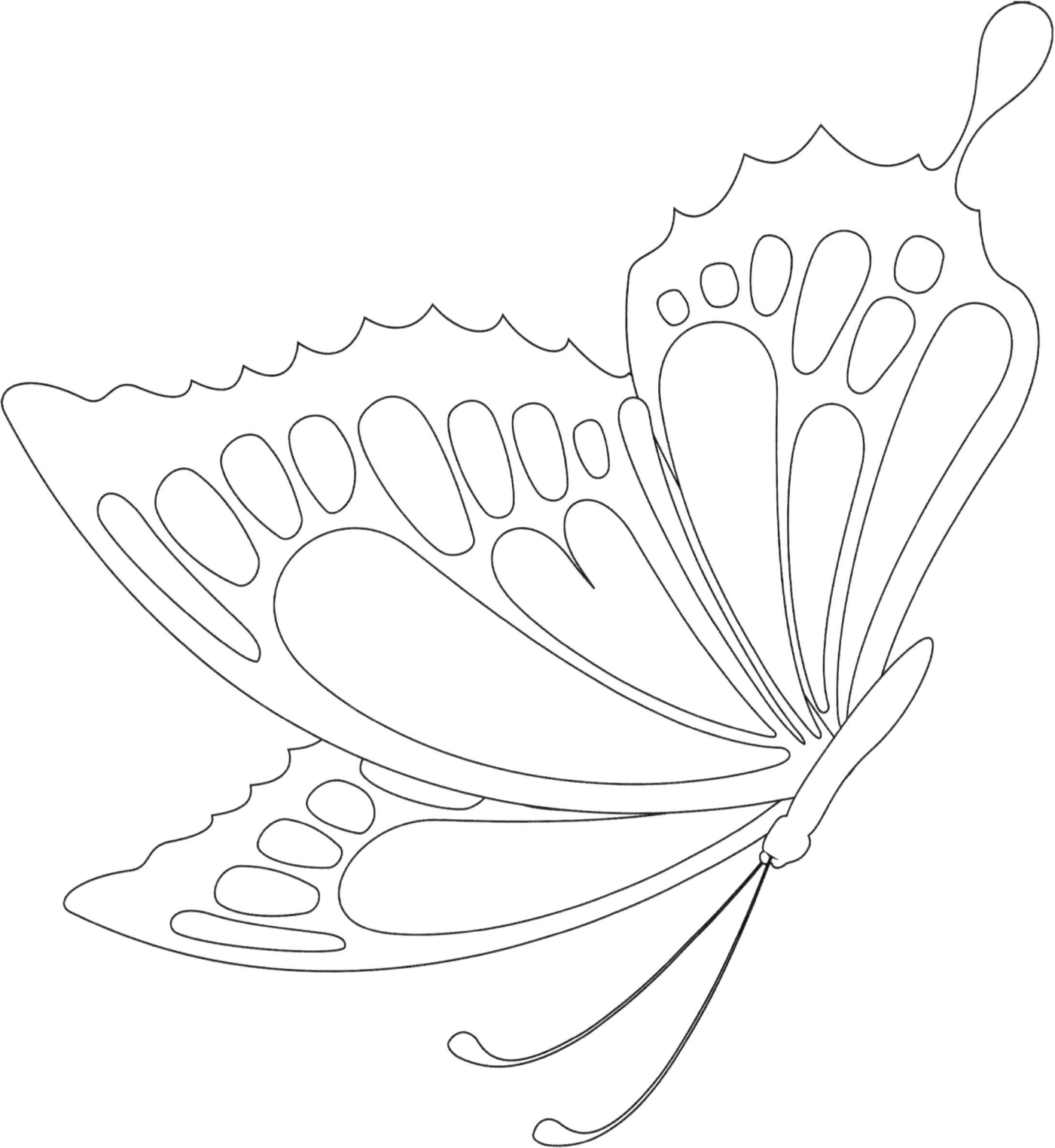

85

Angela

87

Zebra heliconian

Summer

91

Silk maria

Northern brown argus

Eastern comma

Baby butterfly

Glanville fritillary

Acknowledgements

Some images and designs were use with permission from freepik.com

Some images and designs were use with permission from pexels.com

Some images and designs were use with permission from vexels.com

Some images and designs were use with permission from pixabay.com

Some images and designs were use with permission from depositphotos.com

www.ingramcontent.com/pod-product-compliance
Lightning Source LLC
Chambersburg PA
CBHW081648270326
41933CB00018B/3391